Intro

Welcome to "Saint Francis of Assisi: 100 Quotes to Live By"! This little book is packed with wisdom from one of the most beloved saints in history.

St. Francis believed in the power of love, compassion, and humility, and his words still resonate with us today. So whether you're a devout follower or just someone looking for a little inspiration, this book is for you.

Inside, you'll find 100 of St. Francis's most inspiring quotes, each one carefully chosen to help you live your best life. So go ahead, flip through these pages, and let St. Francis guide you on your journey to inner peace and joy.

Edited by David Smith © 2023

1

"Holy charity confounds all diabolical and fleshly temptations and all fleshly fears."

2

"Not to hurt our humble brethren is our first duty to them, but to stop there is not enough. We have a higher mission; to be of service to them whenever they require."

3

"It is no use walking anywhere to preach unless our walking is our preaching."

4

"Where there is charity and wisdom, there is neither fear nor ignorance."

5

"While you are proclaiming peace with your lips, be careful to have it even more fully in your heart."

6

"Where there is discord may we bring harmony. Where there is error, may we bring truth. Where there is doubt, may we bring faith. Where there is despair, may we bring hope."

7

"He who works with his hands and his head and his heart is an artist."

8

"Do few things but do them well,
simple joys are holy."

9

"For it is in giving that we receive."

10

"You cannot all abandon your possessions, but at least you can change your attitude about them. All getting separates you from others; all giving unites to others."

11

"Go out and preach the gospel and if you must, use words."

12

"Where there is injury let me
sow pardon."

13

"Many who seem to us to be the Devil's children will still become Christ's Disciples."

14

"Remember that when you leave this earth, you can take with you nothing that have received--only what you have given."

15

"You can show your love to others by not wishing they were better Christians."

16

"What is it that stands higher than words? Action. What is it that stands higher than action? Silence."

17

"A man sins who wishes to receive more from his neighbor than he is himself willing to give to the Lord God."

18

"All things of creation are children of the Father and thus brothers of man. God wants us to help animals if they need help. Every creature in distress has the same right to be protected."

19

"Men lose all the material things they leave behind them in this world, but they carry with them the reward of their charity and the alms they give."

20

"We must not be wise and prudent according to the flesh. Rather, we must be simple, humble, and pure."

21

"God requires that we assist the animals when they need our help. Each being (human or creature) has the same right of protection."

22

"It would be considered a theft on our part if we didn't give to someone in greater need than we are."

23

"Be patient in trials, watchful in prayer, and never cease working."

24

"Keep a clear eye toward life's end. Do not forget your purpose and destiny as God's creature. What you are in his sight is what you are and nothing more."

25

"It is in pardoning that we are pardoned."

26

"We should never desire to be over others. Instead, we ought to be servants who are submissive to every human being for God's sake."

27

"Most High, all powerful, good Lord, Yours are the praises, the glory, the honor, and all blessing."

28

"Everything in man should halt in awe... Let all the world quake and let Heaven exult when Christ the Son of the living God is there on the altar."

29

"Nor did demons crucify Him; it is you who have crucified Him and crucify Him still when you delight in your vices and sins."

30

"Dear God, please reveal to us your sublime beauty, that is everywhere, everywhere, everywhere, so that we will never again feel frightened."

31

"Because whoever has joined forces with God obtains three great privileges: omnipotence without power, intoxication without wine, and life without death."

32

"Praised be You, my Lord, through those who give pardon for Your love, and bear infirmity and tribulation."

33

"We adore You, O Christ, and we praise You, because by Your holy cross, You have redeemed the world."

34

"Where there is hatred, let me sow love. Where there is injury, pardon. Where there is doubt, faith."

35

"My God and My All!"

36

"Praised be You, my Lord, through Sister Moon and the stars; in the heavens, you have made them bright, precious and fair."

37

"What sublime humility and humble sublimeness, that the Lord of the Universe, the Divine Son of God, should stoop as to hide Himself under the appearance of bread for our salvation! Behold the humble way of God, my brothers."

38

"If God can work through me, he can work through anyone."

39

"Great and glorious God, and Thou Lord Jesus, I pray you shed abroad your light in the darkness of my mind."

40

"Lord, make me an instrument of thy peace. Where there is hatred, let me sow love."

41

"We adore Thee most holy Lord, Jesus Christ, here in all Thy Churches, which are in the whole world, because by Thy holy cross, Thou hast redeemed the world."

42

"Lord, grant that I might not so much seek to be loved as to love."

43

"The world is a great stage on which God displays his many wonders."

44

"It was easy to love God in all that was beautiful. The lessons of deeper knowledge, though, instructed me to embrace God in all things."

45

"Praise be you, my Lord, through our sister, Mother Earth, who sustains and governs us."

46

"Here is one of the best means to acquire humility; fix well in mind this maxim: One is as much as he is in the sight of God, and no more."

47

"Everything in man should halt in awe... Let all the world quake and let Heaven exult when Christ the Son of the living God is there on the altar."

48

"It is not fitting, when one is in God's service, to have a gloomy face or a chilling look."

49

"I am the herald of the great King."

50

"Our hands imbibe like roots, so I place them on what is beautiful in this world. And I fold them in prayer, and they draw from the heavens light."

51

"Heavenly Father, you created all things for your glory and made us stewards of this creature."

52

"O innocent Jesus, having sinned, I am guilty of eternal death, but You willingly accept the unjust sentence of death, that I might live. For whom, then, shall I live, if not for You, my Lord?"

53

"Lord, help me to live this day,
quietly, easily."

54

"The greatest security we can have in this world that we are in the grace of God, does not consist in the feelings that we have of love to Him, but rather in an irrevocable abandonment of our whole being into His hands, and in a firm resolution never to consent to any sin great or small."

55

"Grant me the treasure of sublime poverty: permit the distinctive sign of our order to be that it does not possess anything of its own beneath the sun, for the glory of your name, and that it have no other patrimony than begging."

56

"God, enlighten the darkness of my heart and give me a right faith, a sure hope, a perfect charity, sense and knowledge, so that I may carry out your holy command."

57

"Be patient, because the weaknesses of the body are given to us in this world by God for the salvation of the soul. So they are of great merit when they are borne patiently."

58

"The Lord bless you and keep you. May He show His face to you and have mercy. May He turn His countenance to you and give you peace. The Lord bless you!"

59

"The tree of love its roots hath spread Deep in my heart, and rears its head; Rich are its fruits: they joy dispense; Transport the heart, and ravish sense. In love's sweet swoon to thee I cleave, Bless'd source of love."

60

"And it is in death that we are
born to eternal life."

61

"You call it a sin, that I love the dog above all else? The dog stayed with me in the storm, the man, not even in the wind."

62

"Alms are an inheritance and a justice which is due to the poor and which Jesus has levied upon us."

63

"We should have no more use or regard for money in any of its forms than we have for dust. Those who think it is worth more, or who are greedy for it, expose themselves to the danger of being deceived by the Devil."

64

"A man has only so much knowledge as he puts to work."

65

"You should never praise anyone until you see how he turns out in the end!"

66

"Don't canonize me too soon. I'm perfectly capable of fathering a child."

67

"What could you do to a man who owns nothing? You can't starve a fasting man, you can't steal from someone who has no money, you can't ruin someone who hates prestige."

68

"Grant me the treasure of
sublime poverty."

69

"A cat purring on your lap is more healing than any drug in the world, as the vibrations you are receiving are of pure love and contentment."

70

"Ask the beasts and they will teach you the beauty of this earth."

71

"Our actions are our own; their consequences belong to Heaven."

72

"Study always to have Joy, for it befits not the servant of God to show before his brother or another sadness or a troubled face."

73

"When we pray to God we must be seeking nothing - nothing."

74

"When I think of the happiness that is in store for me, every sorrow, every pain becomes dear to me."

75

"Don't change the world, change worlds."

76

"Holy wisdom confounds Satan
and all his wickedness."

77

"And blessed is he who loves his brother as well when he is afar off as when he is by his side, and who would say nothing behind his back he might not, in love, say before his face."

78

"Woe to those who die in mortal Sin!"

79

"The brave unfortunate are our best acquaintance."

80

"Water is the mirror of nature."

81

"You can only do what the hand of God allows you to do."

82

"What you are looking for is
what is looking."

83

"Be praised, my Lord, through Brothers Wind and Air, and clouds and storms, and all the weather, through which you give your creatures sustenance."

84

"True progress quietly and persistently moves along without notice."

85

"If a superior give any order to one who is under him which is against that man's conscience, although he do not obey it yet he shall not be dismissed."

86

"The measure of love is to love without measure."

87

"Gold hath no lustre of its own. It shines by temperate use alone."

88

"We have been called to heal wounds, to unite what has fallen apart, and to bring home those who have lost their way."

89

"Where there is poverty and joy, there is no greed and avarice."

90

"By the anxieties and worries of this life, Satan tries to dull man's heart and make a dwelling for himself there."

91

"I need no more, I know Christ,
the poor crucified one."

92

"For these, they will receive from the Lord the reward and recompense they deserve."

93

"A single sunbeam is enough to drive away many shadows."

94

"No one is to be called an enemy, all are your benefactors, and no one does you harm. You have no enemy except yourselves."

95

"If you have men who will exclude any of God's creatures from the shelter of compassion and pity, you will have men who will deal likewise with their fellow men."

96

"Hold back nothing of yourselves for yourselves so that He who gives Himself totally to you may receive you totally."

97

"Sanctify yourself and you will sanctify society."

98

"Blessed are those who endure in peace for by You, Most High, shall they be crowned."

99

"All the darkness in the world cannot extinguish the light of a single candle."

100

"Blessed is the servant who loves his brother as much when he is sick and useless as when he is well and an be of service to him."

Made in United States
North Haven, CT
15 October 2024